The One-Minute Parent

(2nd Edition)

By Dana Minney

Table of Contents:

Introduction

Since my twin sons were born nearly nine years ago, I have stacked up piles of books about parenting. I haven't read more than a few pages of any of them.

If you are a parent, you know why. It's because being a mom and having a career takes so much time, I rarely have time to read books. Ironically, I set these books aside for later, for "When I have time," which will probably not be until my boys are grown.

That is why I wrote a short and sweet book to share what I have learned. Reading this book will only take a few minutes of your time.

And you can apply these principles in less than an instant.

No matter how busy or stressed you are, taking one minute to assess, tune into and respond intelligently to your child, will definitely change the course of your day. Over the long-term, minutes like this will add up to change the course of your life.

For many people, their greatest source of pain is the inability to express their needs and desires in an effective way to family members. How well you can manage these connections often determines the quality of your overall life.

Most parents can afford to give their children at least one minute of their attention...especially if it means the difference between relaxed harmony or continuous conflict and chaos.

In the "One-Minute Manager," Ken Blanchard introduces the idea of 'self-leadership'.

He says in order to be successful in our modern economic landscape companies "Need their people to learn to be empowered problem-solvers and decision makers."

It's the same with families. As our society has gotten more complex, loss of traditional family roles, mixed families, and a more prominent role of technology, our old tools for creating healthy family systems are outdated and ineffective.

For example, everything changed for me after my divorce. Before, I thought my boys needed a dad. I thought the only way kids could grow up to be well-adjusted and emotionally fit was to have a mother AND father living together in the same house.

Three years ago when my husband moved overseas, I was worried. How could I raise emotionally and physically healthy sons by myself? Parenting became a top priority. I noticed every moment with my kids made the difference between whether or not my day would flow smoothly, or whether I would feel stressed, overwhelmed and depleted by my family life.

I learned to be quite effective. I love being a mom and nothing gives me greater joy than the love I have in my heart for my boys, and the love I receive from them. This book gives many stories of how to apply the three principles of business leadership in families.

If we take a page from Blanchard's playbook, we learn that self-leadership, is one of the key elements in any healthy organization. He defines it as "Knowing what you need and how to ask for it."
In other words it is communication and collaboration skills that we need more than ever. But how do we learn these skills?

For those of us lucky enough to work for or with a great organization offering top-notch training on these topics we can learn it in the workplace.

What if we could learn these communication skills...skills that would help us have inspiring connections, have the ability to take stock of what we need, ask for it, and most importantly, how to make a contribution to others...in the home?
What I want to share with you are the three basic habits for communication and collaboration that make family systems smooth and harmonious. It is also what makes organizations, events and companies run smoothly.

Here they are:
1) Be honest
2) Have fun
3) Create value

If you take these principles at face value they will make a big difference. But I want to have a heart-to-heart conversation with you, as one parent to another...so we can discover profound knowledge that will make our lives easier and protect the love that we so cherish in our families.

Chapter 1:

Be Honest

Babies are the most honest people alive. Their love and curiosity are so all-encompassing that they are incapable of deceit or manipulation. You are like that too, under most conditions.

If you lie, your kids know it. They will learn to lie too. Then when you lie with good intentions or maybe without even being aware of it, you set in motion a dynamic of dishonesty in your family when you lie.

It becomes kind of like an unwritten rule. Nearly all parents lie to their kids. It almost seems unavoidable! Therefore many families fall into a dynamic of deceit.

Pretending everything is okay when it is not is an innocent lie. But deceit creates damage. Threatening that your child will receive a consequence if he or she does a certain behavior and then not delivering on that consequence when your child does that behavior is also a lie.

Several years ago, I took my boys on a camping trip with another family. It was less than a year after my husband and I had separated. I was still learning how to be a mom to my twin boys, without the everyday presence of their father. My first lesson was on how important it is to have credibility.

On the last day of our camping trip, we were preparing to leave, packing up the car, and planning how the day was to play out.

The grown-ups had kind of a pow-wow out by our cars and we decided not to let the children go over to the playground because it would be too difficult to gather them up when it was time to leave, which was in just a few minutes.

So the children all came over to us (my two boys and the daughter of the other couple) and asked to go to the playground.

I said "No".

The parents of the other girl said "Okay."

When she started to run over to the playground my boys wanted to go with her.
Again, I said "No." They turned right around and calmly helped me load up the car with no fuss.

As we drove off about ten minutes later, the other family was still trying to wrangle and cajole their daughter, who had learned long ago that she could do whatever she wanted, whenever she wanted.

Although she is adorable and talented, such inconsistency has spoiled her. Now her tyranny is a constant source of stress for her parents.

One day she will face a big disappoint-ment when she realizes that noone else in her life is as easy to manipulate as Mommy and Daddy.

My boys have learned that when I say "No" I mean it. I don't have time or energy to have them doubt, argue or manipulate me.

Credibility is key. If I say, "No, you cannot play on the playground," and then change my mind why would they ever listen to me or believe me again?

Many of my clients who I coach in business are also parents. They complain that their kids don't listen and don't obey.

If kids don't obey, it's probably because they are getting mixed messages. Mom and Dad have no credibility because they have a history of not saying what they mean or meaning what they say.

When one of my sons was about three years old, he shoved a toy truck tire up his nose and it got stuck. It was made out of some kind of foam material so when I tried to remove it with tweezers, it just started to crumble and jam further up inside his nasal passage. I gave up trying to get it out and took him to the emergency room.

While we waited our turn, we noticed several other families in the waiting room. For the next 45 minutes I sat transfixed as a father interacted with his daughter. She repeatedly climbed up on the plastic chairs and jumped off.

Each time she did this, he said, "Stop that! I mean it!" Then he said, "This is your last warning!" and when that didn't work, he said, "I'm going to count to three and then you'll be sorry! One...two...three!" And then nothing happened.

Of course the girl continued to climb and jump, climb and jump, climb and jump. Each time she did it it was with greater and greater amounts of defiance.

This girl may never respect her father's word. She could well struggle in life to understand limits and boundaries. But most tragically, she learned that daddy lies.

"This is your last warning." was a lie.

"I mean it." was a lie.

"I'm going to count to three and then you'll be sorry." was a lie.

Now she knows lying is acceptable and, soon, she will begin to lie.

Parents have a running joke, "Do as I say, not as I do." But it just doesn't work that way. Children don't do what we say, they do what we do.

As a single parent the responsibility is doubled. Since no other grownups live in our house for the kids to observe, I am their main model for behavior. Every behavior that my children observe in me becomes a model for my sons to imitate.

I had made mistakes before, of course, but somehow after I became a single parent it seemed my mistakes were suddenly magnified. Everything came back right in my face immediately. Children are great reflections of us, both for our flaws and our genius.

Once I caught myself training my sons not to listen to me. As soon as I realized it, I stopped it immediately and self-corrected! Thank goodness for awareness!

What happened was that they were fighting with each other and making a huge racket. The noise was making me nuts.

I finally lost my cool and started shouting at them, "YOU WILL NOT RAISE YOUR VOICE IN THIS HOUSE IT IS NOT OK FOR YOU TO SHOUT STOP IT RIGHT NOW!!"

Well of course I lost all credibility in that moment because I was breaking my own rule by shouting when I had just said, "Shouting is not okay!"

I showed them, by example, that it IS okay to shout and also therefore, NOT necessary follow the rules.

Do you think I want to teach my children to do what I did? No! But at the time I did not think about what example I was setting for them and how seriously they buy into what they observe.

Next time the boys are loud, instead of shouting at them, I can take a minute and give them my attention.

Once I tune into them, I can calmly acknowledge their noise and calmly acknowledge the effect it has on my nerves. This demonstrates honesty.

After earning their trust with honesty, and from a calm perspective, I can become clear about my next choice. I can choose to give myself a 'time out' in my room. I can put on my earbuds and tune out their noise with music. Or I can choose to dock points and send them outside. My choice to shout out of frustration was the probably the least effective choice! But we must make mistakes to learn.

Chapter 2:

Have Fun

My boys also taught me how important it is to play. Whenever I am playing with my children, they listen to me. But if I get serious or if my demeanor, body language and voice tone indicate that something is wrong, they immediately tune me out.

It would be nice if my kids would just automatically listen to me no matter what. But that's just not the case. So I can choose to be upset about the fact that they don't listen, or I can do something that works.

What works is to play. My sons respond instantly to playfulness. They are a great reminder to me to stay in a playful mood. No matter what the situation, approaching them with a warm heart and light attitude is always more effective than with stress and anger.

Recently, my kids and I took a vacation and stayed with my ex-husband's family in France. It was a totally new environment with very different kinds of people. To make things even more stressful I would be leaving the boys there while I went on a four-week coaching tour of Europe.

So I had 24 hours to train the new caregivers in our family dynamics. I let them know all the no-go foods. Taught everyone about our family ground rules, and showed them how to use natural consequences to maintain order and respect.

It was an overwhelming task! And, needless to say, it wasn't easy bridging the two cultures.

When I tried to talk to the kids and the in-laws with my 'stressed' voice, nobody listened!

In fact, immediately after telling my ex-mother-in-law that the boys earn points every day for doing a kitchen job (either setting the table or clearing the table) she nodded her head, and immediately got up and cleared the table!

At first, I felt very irritated with her. But I then realized that a 68-year-old is just like an 8-year-old! She only listens if it sounds fun.

Well a solution soon emerged. The house we were staying at luckily had a basketball hoop and a trampoline. I quickly discovered that the way to have my children listen, even in a new environment, was to jump on the trampoline or start shooting hoops with them.

We were all having fun when we were bouncing, shooting or both. I could say things to them and they would listen respectfully. When our bodies were playing and when my tone and demeanor were lighthearted, everyone listened.

When my face was pinched with pressure and my voice was tight nobody could hear me.
I am really thankful for my sons for teaching me this lesson. Choosing to have fun rather than suffer is well...much more fulfilling!

Children are always ready to play. Seldom do they need encouragement. In fact, my children are very often good guides for me in having fun. I just follow their lead.

Once I heard a story about a family that played a game where whoever was having the most fun got to be the leader and decide what the family would do as an activity. On a day when I was feeling not-so-fun I decided to try it out.

"Kids," I said. "We are going to play a game. Are you ready? Whoever is having the most fun and including the others in the fun gets to hold this magic wand. When you have the magic wand, you get to decide what activity we do."

Immediately they sprang into action. Laughing and dancing and jumping on the bed (which is against the house rules, by the way.)

"Oops!" I said. "You are doing a great job having fun but you are not including me and you are breaking the house rules!"

One of my sons jumped down and ran over to me, grabbed my hands and started to dance with me. It totally worked!

My spirits lifted as they transported me into playfulness.

"You get the magic wand," I said to him and handed him a fancy pen from my desk.

It happened to be that the son who got the wand was the more self-absorbed and bossy one. I was curious to see what would transpire once I literally handed him the power.

To my surprise, the first thing he wanted to do was please us and makes us happy.

"Mommy," he said. "What do you want right now?"

"I would like to make myself some iced tea," I said.

"Go do that. And once you drank it all, please go make some more for yourself!"
Happily, I obeyed. As I left the room he turned to his brother. "And, what do you want?"

"Watch a movie!" my other son shouted.

"OK! Pick one out and put it in the player."

Soon we were all gathered on the floor with some cushions watching our favorite family movie. Having a great connection made me forget all about the unpleasant things that had happened that day. My children had guided me to fun-world!!

I am lucky because I learned so much from my own family about having fun as a team. My mom, dad and even my brother are natural coaches. I love seeing my sons play with their grandparents and their cousins and uncle.

My dad even created what he calls 'Grampa Camp'. Whenever he is with my boys, he plays games with them and rewards them with points, popsicles or money.

Within the games, he has the children's attention and can teach them things with playfulness. For example, he does soccer drills, plays football, does art projects and other sports. They love Grampa Camp! I love Grampa Camp because I know my children are having fun and learning.

Kids respond to games. In companies this is called 'Game Theory'. A game happens within a specific time frame, with specific rules and with a clear goal or outcome. In this structure, people can unite as a team and experience high performance. Game theory works beautifully with families!

Even with a little bit of initial resistance, children will almost always transcend boredom or inertia when invited to play.

One day when gramma and grampa, my brother, his kids, myself and my boys were together at the park, the kids were being lazy and refused to play. It was a beautiful day and of course we wanted the boys to be active.

My brother stood up and kicked the soccer ball over to me, "Let's play keep- away from the kids." I stood up and kicked the ball back. "Oh, this will be easy!" I said.

As soon as he stated the challenge and kicked me the ball, the kids were up and running. They laughed joyously as they gently shoved into us, trying to steal the ball and then maintain possession of it.

In an instant, they had shifted from flopping and complaining to running and laughing. My brother had initiated the game and...Voila! Suddenly all of our faces were lit with the aliveness and happiness of play. We ran, kicked and sweated in the sunshine for nearly an hour after that. Even Gramma and Grampa joined in the fun!

While my brother's goal was simply to get the kids moving, he accomplished many other positive outcomes as well. Our kids were learning new skills through the play. He created unity, because even though the kids were against the adults, we were all united in play. It was a friendly, family competition.

Most importantly, he shifted the dynamic from low-energy, and low-vitality to high-energy, high-vitality connection. Our communication followed suit. Instead of whining, we heard joyful shouts of, "Pass it to me!", "Good one!", "I'm open!", and "Block Grampa!"

Chapter 3:

Create Value

When my twins were 15 months old, I asked my mentor to share with me what he knew about healthy family systems. I knew that he had spent the first decade of his career in a mental health center as a family systems therapist. Since leaving the clinic he had later moved into the field of coaching where he discovered newer, more effective communication tools.

He gave me a download of his approach for creating

value in a family system. When you appreciate every experience, you teach your children to create value, you teach them respect.

From that we created our Family Reward Program as a point system where each family member earns points based on specific tasks. You can find an outline of our method in Appendix A. You can also find a template of a chart for you to create your own Family Reward Program in Appendix B.

You can customize your game to fit your own family and lifestyle. Be sure to keep it simple. Make it easy for you and your kids to play. And, of course, like any game, it must be FUN!

Every day, I pay my boys at the end of the day based on whether or not they perform certain tasks throughout the day. Having a cooperative attitude is one of the tasks. A good attitude warrants points earned (or docked, as the case my be.)

Some parents object to allowing kids to earn cash. But it works for us. My boys don't have to ask me for everything they want. They learn to make choices on how to earn and how to spend money, wisely.

For example, if one of the boys offers to help me, carrying in groceries, or help his brother find something he has lost, that shows a cooperative attitude.

If one of my boys is not cooperating, I give a verbal acknowledgement two times before implementing the consequence.

Let's say for example, one of the boys is whining. I will say, "You are whining. That is not a cooperative attitude. Use a normal voice and tell me what you want."

Let's say, hypothetically of course, that the whining continues. I say, "This is your second warning. Please stop whining."

Let's say, the whining continues still. I say, "You have lost your cooperation money for today." If the whining continues I ask if they want to go in time out.

It will be clear then whether or not my son chooses to shift his attitude or to take a brief time out. If he still does not shift, I send him into another room, or a separate area--away from us, away from the fun.

Every athlete respects the time-out ritual. If players commit too many fouls, they get to sit out of the game for a specific period of time. Time out gives the player time to chill and to reflect on what happened. I have given my sons time-outs at the supermarket, at parties and in airports. I maintain credibility with them this way.

The boys know if I say they will get a time out, they will get a time out. And I am not worried about strange looks I get from bystanders. Actually, people are usually quite impressed to see how calmly I handle the situation without punishing, getting mad, or making the child wrong.

During time-out sessions, I shift my attention away. But I stay nearby. In public (for example at an airport), I do not want to stray too far from my child!

Attention is a reward, just as points are. I am lucky that I have two children. I can shift my attention to the twin who is not being a problem. Since our household emphasizes fun together I can give lots of attention and acknowledgment to whoever is lightest.
Soon the reluctant son will want to join in. Because having fun as a family team is...well; more fun!

Having the task list and point system makes it very clear what value I expect each of the boys to deliver and what value they will receive when they do it.
If they don't perform their tasks they don't earn their points for that task for the day. It is a simple system.
They create value for themselves by deciding how much value they produce that day.

Each one can decide for himself what he earns by what he does.

You can compare this approach to leadership training. In the book, "The One-Minute Manager" Ken Blanchard refers to it as 'self-leadership'. A leader does not wait for a handout or whine until something happens. A leader decides what he or she wants to do and then does it and takes the consequences.

What also works about this system is that there is no punishment. I don't have to get mad or take personal offense when my children make decisions how to behave. Like a fair referee, I simply deliver the consequence.

My guys have been immersed in this cause and effect environment for practically their whole life so it has become second nature to them. That is why our family enjoys great times nearly all the time.

When I first introduced natural consequences parenting, I was afraid it wouldn't work. I thought, "My kids are not interested in money. They don't even know what money is!"

I was prepared to go into a long explanation about what money is and how you can use it to buy things that you want. So I also had a backup plan in case they weren't interested. I was going to offer them stickers or tiddly winks or something else. I pulled out the jar of pennies I keep in the kitchen whenever I empty out my purse of spare change.

I held it up and said, "Kids, these are pennies. Ok..." I was just about to launch into my 'what-you-can-do-with-money' speech when they both started to lunge toward me, grabbing at the jar and shouting "MINE-MINE-MINE!!"

Since they could barely walk or talk at this time, it was quite astonishing that they were suddenly motivated to cooperate, simply because they saw some pennies!

In Chapter One, I illustrated how kids don't want to listen to lectures, or any grown up giving instructions, ever.

Kids don't enjoy lectures, instructions, criticism or any other heavy messages delivered by serious and/or cranky grown-ups. However, kids will respond to play-based rules.

Imagine a soccer game where the rules on what is fair and what is foul are clearly agreed upon beforehand. The referee doesn't get mad at the players when they break the rules. He or she simply dishes out the consequence (i.e. a yellow card or a red card) depending on what the player does. The referee is not the one sitting in the stands, or the announcer criticizing the players. He or she is right on the field with them. His intervention guarantees a fair game.

Assuming that all players want to play and win, this system makes the game safe and keeps it running smoothly.

You might want to explore what motivates your kids. It may be time on the computer. It may be a play date with another child or a night out with Mom and Dad at the arcade.

You will need to experiment to find out what works to make your children want to play the cooperation game.

My kids are motivated by money because they can buy toys and gum with it...which they otherwise don't get, because I don't buy those things (except for birthdays and other special occasions).

On a recent plane ride my sons and I sat quietly while the flight attendant went through the whole safety speech and demonstration. After it was over, my son turned to me and said, "Can you show me where the oxygen mask is and how to use it?"

"Weren't you just listening to the instructions?" I asked him.

"No, I don't like lectures, can't you just show me?"
Just then the pilot came on and gave a speech about the weather, the expected turbulence during the flight, and landing time.

As if to demonstrate the point, my other son turned to me when it was over and said with a puzzled look on his face, "Did you just hear something?" I don't know if he was being humorous or serious...and I was afraid to ask!

My kids are not perfect and I am certainly not perfect at parenting but there are a couple things I have done right and their behavior shows it.

Last month my sons got invited to stay with their Gramma and Grampa in San Diego. This was a real treat for them because they only see them about three times a year, and of course time with grandparents is very special to kids!!

Before they arrived I briefed my mom and dad on the system and how we use three warnings before delivering a consequence for a behavior that is not working.

After the two weeks was over I asked my mom how it went and she said 99% of the time it was a pleasure and the system worked very well. They had a lot of fun.

"There was just one time," she said, "when one of the boys decided to have a big, hairy fit because he was not getting his way, and it was his brother who helped him to calm down".

She continued telling the story and said that his brother had said things like, "You already got two warnings so if you don't calm down you won't get your reward!" He also said, "just take a deep breath and think about something you like!"

After a couple minutes his brother had totally calmed down and changed his attitude.

I was a very proud mama at this point. It was a great example of how my children have learned to create value...and even teach it to others.

By walking his brother through the process of calming himself down, he showed everyone in the room, including my Mom and Dad, how to do the same. It was like a 'how-to' demonstration for family harmony.

I have given examples showing the things I am doing right, teaching my children about leadership, choices and creating value.

Believe me, there are also many examples of things I have done and am still doing that don't work.

For example, my children are nearly nine years old and don't tie their own shoes. They rarely brush their teeth without a reminder. Sometimes they have the table manners of complete slobs. This is especially when we are out to dinner or have guests over.

I give myself a break on those issues because I don't want to waste energy trying to be perfect. And I don't want my kids to be perfect or to expect perfection. That would not prepare them for life. Real life is messy. More than anything I want my sons to have tools for acceptance, courage and flexibility for dealing with the unexpected aspects life.

Someone once said, "The most important thing that parents can teach their children is how to get along without them."

I love my children and I know it will break my heart when they fly the nest. But someday they will need to leave me. I want them to go out on their own and make mistakes and make choices that I may find strange and shocking. Meantime I want to help them grow and take responsibility for themselves. It is an honor and a joy to be with them as they develop into fine young men. I treasure each minute.

Part II:

Putting it Into Practice

Part II:

Putting it Into Practice:

Since writing the first edition of the <u>One Minute Parent</u> and working with parents in seminars and webinars all over the world, I have received numerous requests for *real-life* examples.

"Part II: Putting it into Practice" is the answer to your requests. Each story in this section is a true example of how the principals you have read about or learned about in the "How to Coach Your Kids" webinars play out in real life. The stories may come from a client, friend or my own family. Some of the names may have been changed per request.

Please be aware when you read them you may take them as a 'how-to' and copy someone else's actions step-by-step, but you don't have to! Only you know best what will work for you and your family.

Each family has unique characteristics and challenges. By reading about what other moms, dads and caregivers have done, you will hopefully feel empowered to be more creative and take some risks in your family leadership. Coaching is not an exact science and there are no easy answers.

It is my mission when working with parents to give support and encouragement in their efforts to maintain a connection and a collaborative spirit with children. The principles in the One Minute Parent work on the basis of communication and collaboration. Staying in the connection with your family member is key.

Traditional parenting styles work on the basis of domination, manipulation or the permit/punish cycle. These methods may sometimes be effective. But, in the words of my wise friend, Felora, "Punishment may solve the immediate problem, but in the long-term it creates more problems. It only makes you better at hiding your bad actions and it destroys the connection. It also does not change the dynamic that caused the child to act out in the first place."

Staying connected with your child comes naturally when things are easy. But the moment there is a crisis and one of you gets angry or upset, your connection can become threatened. The following examples are inspiring because they show how rewarding it is to stay in the connection, even when it is hard, painful and scary. Because it *is* hard, painful and scary, you need resources like The One Minute Parent.

Please let this book serve as a reminder, rather than a 'how-to' guide, to keep the connection with your child. Staying in the process of connecting is the most important aspect of parenting. I call it a process because sometimes you have a connection, sometimes you don't. Sometimes your connection is strong and sometimes it is weak. If you stay in the dialogue on how to connect, overall you will gain a stronger and stronger connection.

Chapter 1:

Staying Connected Even if it's Hard

Jake's Story

"Since I am a guy, it was difficult when my daughter Zoe turned 13. I really did not know how to talk to her and there were extenuating circumstances that affected my ability to concentrate on her. My work, sick mother, sick brother...all these things required my attention.

"During elementary school she always had lots of friends and lots to do, but things changed in middle school. She started to have more arguments with her friends, and she started to have more problems with her schoolwork. It was a hard time for me and I did the best that I could. But things just seemed to get worse.

"She was having trouble with math, so I tried to help her with homework. That was a disaster! I found I had little patience with her. I would get mad, telling her to 'Pay attention, dammit, quit getting up to do something else every five seconds.' She would get frustrated and start crying, 'I'm trying, quit yelling at me!'

"I was not aware of attention deficit disorder, so I thought that she was just being obstinate. Finally, she would just run into her room, telling me she would just get tutoring at lunchtime. This was just what I wanted to hear. What I did not know is that her teachers were not allowing her to get tutoring, and they were not helping her either. They treated her as if she was being willful as well.

"Then that led to more trouble. She started to fake being sick to miss school and she got a boyfriend (not what a father wants to hear.) Her boyfriend was a marijuana user and I caught Zoe with drug paraphernalia. Fireworks ensued. Then she got caught with her boyfriend shoplifting, and I found out she was taking my car out at night.

"With each new infraction, I would yell at her and tell her she was grounded, and she would get mad and cry and go to her room. Then one night I accused her of doing drugs and that I was convinced that she was hooked on something. She went yelling and crying to her bedroom and slammed the door.

"All of a sudden, I had some sort of awakening or moment of clarity or something, and I could see myself when I was 13 and considered suicide. Being 13 is just not that easy, and I was not helping things, in ways that I did not even realize. It all just came rushing back...I realized that Zoe was going through what I had gone through and that she needed me to help her through this. My suicidal thoughts had come and gone and never came back. I knew it would probably be the same for her, and that everything would eventually turn out fine.

"In that moment, everything changed. I went into her room and hugged her and told her that I loved her and no matter what I would always love her and that I was here to help her. She started sobbing and just started to talk to me. I remember her saying, 'It is so frustrating to be yelled at and be told how horrible I am, when I am the only one of my friends that refuses to do drugs and I am trying so hard at school, but I cannot understand the work and the teacher just tells me that she does not have time to teach me and to quit asking questions, and that I should just ask someone next to me to help but they do not understand either.'

"I remember how awful it was when I was doing my best and I was accused of not trying. Nothing is more disheartening. Think how many arguments and heartache would be avoided if only all parents can remember what it was really like to be 13.

"I realize now, that for one thing she needed glasses, and that she has a hard time concentrating for long periods of time on one thing. But I also learned that she can be a hard worker and she is actually very smart. She is doing very well in math now and has written inspiring letters. We have enrolled her in an alternative charter school that she seems to like much better. She still has trouble with friends, but we are working on it. I know now that helping her is my most important job.

"Now she has a part-time job that she loves, she will graduate soon from High School and is looking at colleges. Things aren't perfect, because life isn't perfect. But we are connected and she is always willing to move forward, to keep trying. Friends tell me that it is my belief in her that gives her the courage and desire to keep trying. So many other girls take a really destructive path during those difficult middle school years, or they just give up. That is a tragedy. So far our life is not a tragedy…because I had the courage and insight to step in and intervene in a very loving way."

Felora's Story:

My dear friend Felora is a great mom and wise woman. Recently she told me a story about when her daughter was a teenager going through a rebellious stage.

"My daughter was acting out and in some cases her behavior was very extreme. I was very afraid of losing my daughter. In the past, I never relied on punishment with my kids. Instead, I always focused on rewarding them with passes or activities when they were cooperative and doing well. One day, we caught my daughter doing something against our family rules. When my husband and I found out, she tried to avoid talking to me about it. She came home and locked herself in her room. I knocked on her door and told her I needed to talk to her. She refused. I said, 'ok. Whenever you're ready I need to talk to you before you leave the house.'

"Later she chose to come out and talk to me. In that conversation, I told her 'I'm not going to punish you because you're old enough to face the consequences on your own of what you did. But I wanted to talk to you because I need to tell you that this behavior is not you. I have known you since you were born. I know you and I see who you are. You have always been kind and considerate. I have witnessed how you have helped other kids out of trouble. When they needed a shoulder to cry on, you were there for them. You always wanted the best for others and now I want the best for you. I want you to remember who you are.'

"I wanted her to know that I still accept her and I still love her and it's hard to be standing by and watching other influences determine her behavior. I wanted to remind her who she is. At that moment it was important for me to keep my connection with my daughter.

"Since that day our connection has gotten better and better. She's no longer acting out and she calls or texts me every couple of days and replies immediately whenever I reach out to her even though she is away at college and very busy.

"Teenage years are hard. The kids need to test the limits. It is a turning point. I could have lost her if I had responded with judgment or rejection. What I did was respectfully give her a clear reflection of herself so she can connect back to who she is, and then decide how to behave. I was able to keep the connection because I am adaptable. I could have lost her but I didn't. I'm very grateful."

Chapter 2:

Natural Consequences

A natural consequence is what happens as a result of a child's choice. Natural consequences give a child a sense of ownership and power about their actions. Letting a child experience natural consequences for their behaviour teaches him or her accountability in preparation for adulthood. Allowing consequences to help your child learn and grow makes your job of parenting easier.

The sooner you allow your child to see and feel the impact of his or her own actions, the sooner your child will have the confidence to take leadership in her life. It can be difficult to deliver a consequence that allows the child to experience the impact of his or her choice without punishment. Here's a simple rule of thumb to tell the difference between natural consequences and punishment. A consequence should be related, respectful and reasonable.

With natural consequences, you provide choices for the child within firm limits and give the child a sense of power. Punishment, on the other hand, is designed to control behavior. It often causes pain and/or humiliation and is delivered with anger (or fighting words). For a clear distinction on the difference between punishment and logical consequences, please refer to Appendix C.

The practice of giving natural consequences within safe and firm limits is key to bringing a coaching perspective into your parenting. In sports, a coach's job is to let consequences rather than punishment stimulate the player to improve his or her skills in the game.

When I was a girl I played softball. In this and the other sports I played it allowed for me to learn many skills, mainly accountability to a team. One year I had a coach whose ground rule was do not miss warm-ups before a game or you do not get to play.

One time, I missed warm-ups and showed up just before game time. My coach was very serious but kind when he delivered the news that I would be sitting on the bench that day.

"Dana, I was very clear about the rules." He said to me sadly. I could see it hurt him to bench me. For one thing, he knew I loved the game and that it would be painful for me to not play. For another thing, it meant the backup first baseman (with less experience) would be playing in my place and that could jeopardize our chances of winning.

We lost that game. I have never regretted a decision so much in my life. Boy did I learn my lesson! I was never late to another warm up!

How I knew it was not punishment is that the consequence was not designed to injure or humiliate me and it was not delivered with anger. It was immediate and reasonable. I was not benched the entire season, just one game. That makes sense.

A punishment by definition is something that causes 'suffering as retribution...' Inflicting suffering causes backlash and retaliation. In this case, a punishment would be if I had to run 30 laps or if the coach screamed and threw a bat at me. That would be designed to hurt and shame me and would lead me to have resentment and a desire for retaliation. But it was not like this. To this day I love that coach for what he taught me and how he treated me with respect, even when giving out the consequence.

After that, I wanted to give him my best, to play my heart out. Sitting on the bench made me more determined to play hard and contribute to my team.

Coaching is at its best when that is the result. When you deliver a consequence with firm limits and love in your heart, your player (child) will only want to do better next time, to give you his or her best.

Richard's Story

If you are in doubt about what could be a sane and firm natural consequence, you can ***ask your child***. Even though I am not a parenting expert, I know effectiveness when I see it, and I take note!

A couple years ago I attended an event for kids and families to encourage learning. My two boys were with me along with one of their friends. His mom couldn't attend but she gave me a warning that he needed to take his medicine at lunchtime. I asked what his medicine was for and she listed four or five different conditions including Autism, schizophrenia, and mild Turret's. With some reservations I lead the three boys to one of the sessions on the topic of money. The facilitator wanted to lead the kids in a game where they could learn about spending and earning.

My sons' friend (let's call him Richard) was being quite disruptive. The teacher asked him several times to stay calm. He promised he would. Then, she asked him what did he want to happen if he didn't stay calm. The room went completely quiet. Richard thought about it.

Since he wasn't answering, she asked again, "There must be something that you want to happen if you disrupt the room again. What is that?"

"If you have to remind me again to be quiet then you can move me to another table by myself." She said "ok" and went on with the lesson. After a few minutes, Richard shouted out something in a loud voice. She said, "Ok, please move to that table." He did.

He had a few more mild outbursts, but for the most part was quiet for the rest of the lesson. Since he was by himself at the table, his outbursts were much less disruptive than they were before. He knew exactly what he needed. The teacher was brilliant to collaborate with the boy to create his own consequences. That way, he really got the impact of his decision. Because he was the one who had created it!

Dana and Jakob's Story:
One day, Jakob and Johannes and myself were out and about at the mall and when we got home Jakob said, "Oh my gosh! I lost my money!" He had had a painted can that he used as a piggy bank with about $10 in it and it was gone.

He said, "Can you go get it Mommy?"

I said, "No, your money is your responsibility." He started to cry and get very upset. "How will I get it back?" he wailed. I asked him when did he last remember having it. We went back through a list of all the places we had visited and he tried to remember if he had his money can at each place.

Finally, he remembered having it at the last place we were at (Starbucks at the mall) and did not remember having it after that.

"Can we go there now?" he asked hopefully. I said "No, now I'm tired."

He started to look panicky and weepy again and said, "What if it's there and someone else takes it! Can you call them and find out if they have it?"

Again, I said, "No, it's not my money and not my job call them."

"Then I need to call them?"

I said, "Yes."

"Can you look up their phone number?"

"I'll show you how to look up their phone number." I said. So we went online and I showed him how to type the name of the place he was looking for. He did that and found the phone number and called them on the phone. The person who answered was very kind and said, "Jakob! We've been waiting for you to call! We have your piggy bank right here and it has your name on it!"

He covered the mouthpiece to whisper excitedly to me, "They have it!"

He asked them to hold onto it for him and they agreed. Of course he wanted to leave immediately. I told him we had to go when it fit with our schedule. I said we could go on Fri. When we entered the café, he walked confidently up to the counter while his brother and I stood outside. When he introduced himself, the cashier smiled and pulled out the can. It was a lesson well learned. He has never lost his money since!

Gina's Story

A colleague of mine who also has twins has raised her girls with coaching principles. They are now 30 and each following a successful career path very well suited to their unique qualities. During Middle School years my friend faced a frustrating situation where allowing 'natural consequences' to do the work for her, turned out beautifully.

"My girls have and always have had very different personalities. When they were in Middle School I used to pick them up after school. One daughter always came promptly out to the car and was ready to go. The other daughter would linger and talk to her friends and teachers and sometimes took up to 45 minutes! It was not fun for my other daughter and I to sit in the car while she conducted her social hour.

"I told her it didn't work for us to wait for her after school and next time I was going to leave without her if she was not ready to go after school. I went to a cab company and interviewed cab drivers until I found one who was honest and trustworthy. I made the deal with him that if he received a call from my daughter he should come to the school and pick her up and deliver her home. I gave him the address of the school and our home. I also gave my daughter the number of the cabdriver and instructed her to call him if needed.

"The next day, when it was time to go after school, one daughter was there and the other daughter was not. We left for home without her. About an hour later we saw my daughter pull up in the cab. After that, she was never late again!

Gina later explained, "The natural consequences journey is a REALLY good one. It's helped me in business, as well as with the child rearing. When there are clearly communicated guidelines that people agree to, then the consequences of actions--for the good or bad--become simply 'what's so' and the emotional charge can be released. Everyone is freed up to choose as they like."

Chapter 3:

How Games Bring Fun and Accountability

In the first edition of the <u>One Minute Parent</u> and in the "How to Coach Your Kids" webinars, I talk a lot about games. Many parents have asked for more details about what is a game and how do you create one. More importantly, why is it so important?

A very simple answer to this last question is that without a game there is no team. Without a team there is no opening to play the role of a coach. If you want to bring coaching tools and the fresh, fun outlook of coaching to your family system, you must have a game. You will also need the willingness to adapt and create new games each time one is completed.

A game has three elements: 1- a challenge, 2- a specific outcome within a time limit and 3- a reward or celebration at the end. Games bring excitement and cooperation through play.

A great example happened over a recent Christmas holiday because of my brother and his wife who are both very competitive and love games. Every member of our family received a present that somehow had a written clue inside it. Each clue was one word. For example, my word was 'in' and next to it was a picture of a diamond then '-MO' and then 'D=?' After all the presents were unwrapped, all of us had to decipher our clues, turn them into words and then put our words together to form a sentence.

Immediately, my brother and his wife had given the

two elements of the game by creating a challenge (figuring out the clues) and the promise of a reward (opening the present once we found it). We came up with the sentence by working together. It was, 'Do you see a big strong Indian?"

We looked around and found a picture of an Indian with a clue written on the back. It told us where to find the next clue. Immediately we all (5 grown-ups and 4 kids) ran to get the next clue and on and on until finally we were led outside to a bigger package. The children grabbed it victoriously and began to rip it open. It was tickets for all of us to go see the Cirque du Soleil show on the following Saturday.

In the moments that we were on the hunt for the gift we were all a team. We were cooperating as equals and we were all working together. It was the high point of our present opening. That's what games can do.

The Fittest Family Contest: A Game for the Whole Community

Children naturally want to play, to give and receive attention. As we grow older we learn to override these natural impulses. Instead of playful ease in communication, like we all had when we were children, we turn into adults who use expression as a war of words and a struggle to establish dominance.

If you can somehow become as curious as you were when you were a child, you are well on your way to creating healthy (socially, physically and emotionally) human beings. Rediscover how to really tune in, with a light and loving heart, to your loved ones. Watch how it restores the spirit of childlike cooperation, team spirit in your family connections.

Three years ago, I joined the PTA of my sons' elementary school. I was recruited to join the Executive Board as the Healthy Lifestyles Chair. With my background in game theory and communication, I know that the secret to physical health is an emotionally safe home life and loving family dynamics.

Understanding this lead me to create a yearlong program bringing families into a spirit of playful cooperation. The program centered on various events where families were required to participate together in different types of challenges, games and learning opportunities. Then they received rewards and prizes (as a family) for participating.

A side effect was that many people actually began to lose weight and change what they ate simply by participating as a team with their family in a more active life.

And a direct effect was that families that previously had stress or anger in their system became playful and light-hearted. They began to create new emotional bonds that went deeper than any fad, nutrition lesson, or any other educational program designed to change people's behavior around health. Families were working (or playing) toward a common goal, which served as a productive distraction from focusing on their problems.

Now, the program has been taken up by numerous other schools, it is still going strong at my sons' school and has been recognized by the National and Texas PTA as a Best Practice for Healthy Lifestyles and Family Engagement.

And it's all about play! It's really as simple as that.

Chapter 4:

How to Create Value

Most kids want appreciation and validation even more than new toys or candy (which you know they love!) If you give them real ways to experience giving and being recognized for a contribution you can benefit in many ways.

Rather than reinforcing a pattern of taking and taking (and taking...), you can teach your young people a new perspective. You can call it 'contributing', 'team spirit' or simply 'being a good family member'. Part of the socialization process (socialization means teaching kids habits and behaviors that help them get along with other people) is to demonstrate productive behaviors and then reward your children when they exhibit these behaviors. Learning to contribute to other people's happiness is a wonderful quality to reinforce in your child. And, it makes them much more fun to live with if they know how to give back, rather than just take what you give them.

The clearest method for rewarding your child is to give the reward immediately and in the form of something he or she recognizes as valuable (for example: candy, toys or money). Earlier I acknowledged even if you object to giving material things to reward behavior that you expect your kids to automatically do, *it just really does work*! Trust me! You can call it bribery, but that's not what it is. If you put a system in place for kids to create value in exchange for value, you create conditions for ongoing cooperation.

Bribes and threats are alike in that they are both manipulations invented on the fly to get a kid to do what you want in the moment. Bribery is a stopgap desperate measure. It may work in the short-term, but in the long run causes more problems. Creating value is different from bribery in that it is an **agreed-upon system established in advance**.

Maureen and Faith's Story

My friend and client Maureen, an entrepreneur, has a great story of how she is teaching her daughter to create value by earning money.

"My 10-year-old daughter Faith has assisted me several times in my business projects and it has not always worked out. Sometimes she would suddenly decide she didn't want to cooperate. This really caused havoc in the projects and was embarrassing in front of my clients.

"Recently, I did a new project where I photographed families in a really fun and silly atmosphere. It required a very special kind of assisting, both technical and theatrical and encouraging. I didn't want to take any chances of her pulling her 'diva' act in the middle of it so I hired her as director. She was paid to do her job and she was great at it! She gave clear instructions, was supportive of our subjects during the shoot and even helped with some of the technical aspects of uploading the photos. I had never seen her be so incredibly helpful with such consistency. She was in the game until the last client walked out the door. There was no scene stealing or ruining the game this time! I loved paying her and seeing how she expressed this new level of leadership. She made a tremendous contribution to my business that day. When I as the parent am clear about the rules and rewards, everything works so much better!"

Chapter 5:

Parenting and Self-Love

Pain and pressure limit our ability to be loving and generous with our children. If you are a mom, the most important thing you can do to mitigate the effects of the pain and pressure of everyday life is to **let yourself get the nurturing you need**. It's your responsibility and no one else's. You must learn to love and nurture yourself the best you can. Don't expect anyone else to do this for you, because they may not know how or they may have other priorities. So get good at giving yourself nurturing and then learn how to ask for it from other people too. Why is this especially important for mothers?

In Gloria Steinem's book, <u>Revolution from Within</u>, she says "people seemed to stop punishing others or themselves only when they gained some faith in their own unique, intrinsic worth." If by 'stop punishing' she means to be more kind and loving. And if by 'faith in their own unique intrinsic worth' she is referring to self-esteem, it follows that women with high self-esteem or self-love are going to be kinder and more loving to their children. So, an open heart is key to being a good mom. And, in order to keep your heart open, be good to your heart.

Here is a delightful story from Heike in Hamburg about how nurturing herself created a wonderful flow of love with her family.

Heike's Story:

"It is the end of a long and successful workshop day. A small but sweet group of women – now all walking out of the door, fulfilled, and tired. Ahhh, I love my work – and feel a bit tired, too. Time to clean up my practice rooms. I move some of the chairs, blow out a candle...the house is still quiet, and my husband has taken the kids ice-skating. And I have a better idea. A radical idea: I am NOT cleaning up my rooms. For now I leave them as is...

"I walk myself to the upstairs bathroom, let hot water flow into the bath tub, turn off the big light, light one big, bright candle, and let myself be surrounded and touched by silence, hot water and candle light. Ahhhhh!

"If you are a mom you know that mostly these moments don´t last forever. After about five minutes into my bath, I heard the door open, and little feet padding the stairs. Both my kids pop their heads into the bathroom – they stop in surprise: 'Wow, Mama, what's going on in here? It looks so cozy and comfortable, what's happening?'

"'Well, I am enjoying myself!' I answered, and so far I really hadn't quite understood the full magic and true meaning of these words.
"My son, very calm and politely, asked me if he could join the bath. He just wanted to be a part of this!! My daughter briefly looked at my feet – that were currently dangling over the edge of the tub, as the water was still steaming hot just the way I like it – and asked me, 'Mama, do you have some oil? I would like to massage your feet – do you want that?'

I am taken by surprise by the sweet offers of the moment – and told her 'Yes!! There is some oil in the drawer of my night stand!!'

"As I am enjoying the hot water, the candlelight, the calm sweetness of my kids AND the foot-massage – my HUSBAND knocks at the door, a little plate with pickles in his hands, PICKLES!

"'Here, this is for starters – I am preparing dinner for all of you right now!' he says.

"I am WOWED by my whole family, and filled up with even more joy, pleasure and gratitude. I am thinking that it seems to make everybody around me very happy to see me relaxed and in pleasure. 'Hey,' I think to myself, 'if all this is what I get for NOT cleaning up my room I wonder why in the world I spend so much energy cleaning up and watching out for everybody else!'

"To all the parents out there, especially the stressed out moms, I highly recommend: Go take a bath and ENJOY!!!!

Chapter 6:

Parenting by Design

My Parent's Story:

My parents are my first and best example of conscious parenting. Neither one of them was an expert when they met in High School many years ago. However, they knew enough about what kind of parents they DIDN'T want to be. It was important enough to both of them to open up a dialogue with each other, even before they started going steady. The quotes below are from a recent retelling of what they knew way back then about the kind of parents they wanted to be.

Mom: "There were things our parents did that we thought were not good to do for children. We wanted: no sarcasm, no flying into a rage when something went wrong, and to stay aware of how our actions impacted the kids."

Dad: "What we knew we did want was to have open communication so that we could talk with our kids and they would feel comfortable talking to us. We wanted to use positive reinforcement rather than punishment. We wanted to encourage conversation at the dinner table. Eating together was important...not always successful but still important."

Mom: "We wanted toys that built self-esteem and encouraged learning. We had special times we called 'kids' night' where we did different things together like cooking, music and crafts."

Dad: "We made some mistakes but overall..."

Mom: "It worked."

Dad: "We have two successful and well-adjusted kids that are now raising kids of their own."

Here is one last note for the <u>One-Minute Parent</u>. It may take an extra minute to think and respond intelligently to your child and to follow these three guidelines, but that minute will make the difference in your family harmony--now and for all the years to come.

In the Introduction I mentioned how much I would love to have a meaningful conversation with you where we can share information. Please feel free to find me on the web at www.HowToCoachYourKids.com or Dana@DanasMyCoach.com.

You are also invited to join a 'How to Coach Your Kids' webinar or subscribe to receive monthly videos, stories and attend the webinars for free. I would love to hear your parenting challenges, stories, and solutions.

Appendix A:
Family Reward Program

Every day, each of the boys have six tasks and receive money at the end of the day based on whether or not they perform the tasks. Each task is worth 10 points (or in our case 10 cents). They have the potential to earn 60 cents per day for six tasks.

Below are the tasks. Please note that this is based on their age, development level and what is needed for our lifestyle to run smoothly. Over the years, the specific tasks have changed to fit our needs and their abilities. You decide what is important for you and your household.

Here are the tasks:

1. Get dressed and be ready to leave the house on time. If it is a school day, that means 7:30am. On a weekend, I let them know ahead of time when we need to be ready by, depending on what is on the

day's agenda. For example, if we have an event at 10am, I will give them a heads up as soon as they wake up that we need to leave by 9:45am, and then give them 30 minute warning, 10 minute warning, etc. If they are not ready to go, they do not earn their money for that task for that day. And, whatever state of dress or undress they are in, is how they need to go. Most of the time, both boys are ready to leave, even if they have to put their shoes on in the car or finish their banana as we are pulling out of the driveway. This is a natural consequence to being late.

2. Do a kitchen job at each meal (either set or clear the table). As I briefly mentioned in Chapter 1, whoever is in charge of setting the table takes everything to the table, including dishes, silverware drinks and plates of food. If they do not come in when I call them to say it is time to set the table, they do not get their money.

To add a challenging twist, if this happens, the other son can step in and to the job, as well as his own job, clearing the table, to earn extra points.

3. Do homework.

4. Read out loud for 15 minutes.

5. Pick up after yourself.

6. Have a cooperative attitude. This is my favorite ground rule because it can be used at any time, in any situation. My boys and I talk about what a cooperative attitude is so they understand specific behaviors.

   For example, if one of the boys offers to help me, carrying in groceries, or help his brother find something he has lost, that is a cooperative attitude.

Appendix B:

Daily Point Chart

	Child 1	Child 2	Child 3	Child 4	Child 5
Task 1					
Task 2					
Task 3					
Task 4					
Task 5					
Task 6					

Appendix C: Punishment vs. Logical Consequences: *What's the Difference?*

*Excerpt from Jim Fay & Charles Fay, Ph.D., Love and Logic Institute, Inc.

Logical Consequences	Punishment
Teach	Control
Leave the student with a feeling of control	Leaves the student feeling helpless
Uses thinking words	Uses fighting words
Provides choices within firm limits	Demands compliance
Are given with empathy	Is given with anger
Are tied to the time and place of the infraction	Is arbitrary
Are similar to what would happen to an adult in a comparable situation	Is arbitrary
Are never used to get revenge	May be used to get revenge (ie. he had it coming!)
Teaches students to take responsibility for their choices	Results in the student focusing on the adult delivering the punishment rather than on their choices